MW00947302

Through My Eyes

By

Kartaysa T. Berry Harris

© 2002 by Kartaysa T. Berry Harris. All rights reserved.

No part of this book may be reproduced, stored in a retrieval system, or transmitted by any means, electronic, mechanical, photocopying, recording, or otherwise, without written permission from the author.

ISBN: 1-4033-6666-7 (e-book)
ISBN: 1-4033-6667-5 (Paperback)

Library of Congress Control Number: 2002111776

This book is printed on acid free paper.

Printed in the United States of America
Bloomington, IN

Cover Design Inspired by Kartisha Harris

E-mail Address ThroughMyEyes@att.com

1stBooks - rev. 12/13/02

This book contains true testimonies of the life of its author. The stories contain specific portions of her personal struggle and deliverance from opposing forces in nature. Which make known her experiences, opinion, and feelings put into word, with details indicating that the need of spiritual support, guidance, and a solid spiritual family foundation are an essential need for teenagers of today.

Her story maybe used as an example for spiritual encouragement to its readers.

All the stories associated in this book are true, however most of the names have been changed to protect the privacy of the people mentioned.

Verses mentioned are taken form the King James Version of the Bible.

iv

Acknowledgments

To my loving husband who has supported me through our good and difficult times, I will love you forever. I know how withdrawn I was throughout the completion of this book. Thank you for your understanding ways and support.

To my beautiful children, the Lord so graciously blessed me with; I love you with all my heart. When I look at each of you, you all are a reminder to me of how awesomely great and merciful my Heavenly Father is.

Many thanks to my loving parents Mr. and Mrs. Berry who are responsible for my very being. There is untold love in my heart for both of you.

To Pastor Hawkins, May God shower you with his "Blessings"; I will never forget what you taught me.

To the Purity Class "Puritans/Trail Blazers"
I have genuine love & concern for all of you and this book shall explain why.

Thanks to my brothers and sisters in Christ for your continued support as I progressed through the completion of this book, which has often times been difficult and challenging. Your prayers have been greatly appreciated.

THROUGH MY EYES

In dedication to my Lord God and Savior Jesus Christ, who sent the Holy Ghost: For His infinite love, grace, and mercy shown toward my life.

TABLE OF CONTENTS

Preface

"Now faith is the substance of things hoped for,
the evidence of things not seen" (Hebrews 11:1).

First I would like to say I'm not telling my story for personal praise or glory, for all praises, glory, and honor belong to God. To those of you who want to feel sorry for what happened to me, don't, that's not the purpose either. **For Jesus has made me free!** I'm only following the path that God has laid out for my life, "It's a Ministry." It is a compelling obligation on my behalf to make known the deliverance power of God. My desire is that you see how I was given divine favor and that many teenagers will come to realize that there is no other way to fill the empty voids in there lives, except through Christ Jesus. Now you make the decision, will you be made free?

This testimonial story was written to encourage one to grasp a hold on Courage, that enduring willingness to face obstacles and deal with evil, anguish, torment, or pain. Embrace Hope, that persevering confidence, firm belief, trust, and reliance on God's certainty assurance, Faith.

My prayer for you is that the Lord will bless you to receive deliverance, that feeling of being freed, total sovereignty spiritually, mentally, emotionally, and physically, just as I have through sharing this story. And above all, that you will retain Hope against Hope, meaning continue to have hope though it seems to have no foundation in reality; no truth in intellectual perception, and is visually unproven. Knowing within your uttermost spiritual being that God is more than able.

I apologize for my explicit straightforward tone. Just know that I can not help you unless I share my experiences in their entirety and explain the mental, physical, and spiritual punishment involved. So, that you may in turn relate your circumstances and feelings. Then I'll make plain through select scriptures how God never intended for you to suffer as his child. However, many trials through your flesh must be sustained in order for you to grow and mature spiritually and obtain his ultimate promise through his son Jesus Christ.

God's plan in accordance to his word instructs us on how we should handle our selves and in him it is possible for us to walk in total freedom over all attachments associated with our natural and spiritual dilemmas.

My approach of resolution is aggressive, but that is what it will take to save our youth. They want someone to be real with them, someone who is not ashamed to say, "I have been were your are, I have even done worse, I can relate because I have felt your pain, and I fell too. God forgives, He forgave me, and because of His grace and mercy He has allowed me to live so that I can help spread His gospel telling youth, 'living saved is the best way'."

Introduction

$\mathcal{A}$s I set wondering, what will I do with the rest of my life? I thought; "How can I help someone else? What purpose did the incidents in my life serve? How can they help others?" I periodically thought on this until I one day heard the spirit of the Lord say, "Write it down, write it down." I tried writing but I stopped. My desire and willingness to venture backward into my past departed from me.

It has been one year and the urging desire and aspirating will power have returned unto me. Today is Nov. 5, 1998, I have been thinking on this for the last four to five days and I have just taken the initiative to act on what the Holy Spirit has given me. Within my uttermost being I feel this sense of urgency. Young people really need to know God, Jesus and what He promises to do for those who love Him and are call for his service.

If it is God's will, by the time you end this partial autobiography you will know portions of my life and come to recognize that as we all travel through this life: Each and every enjoyable, distressing or oppressing event happens for a special reason.

I asked my self, "Is there anything to hard for God?" The Holy Ghost answers back, "There is nothing to hard for God, with man it is impossible but not with God. For all things are possible with God; (forgiveness, healing, deliverance, open doors, love, peace, joy, and all good things) ONLY BELIEVE!"

As I thought on what the Holy Spirit said, I was reminded of how God followed and carried me all throughout my youth before salvation and during my backsliden state. It's quite remarkable to think back and remember God's omnipotent compassion during my teenage years.

Perhaps my story will exemplify the type of unequivocal love and compassion GOD has for all of His children. So, from this moment on, just forget you have eyes and begin to see through mine. I'm serious! Relax and take this amazing journey with me through the pages of... My Life.

Chapter One

Kartaysa T. Berry Harris

My Family

*T*hrough My Eyes, as a child I was not brought up under

Christian Standards. If you would ask my siblings they would say I

was spoiled, fat, and a brat, because I was the baby of the family. To

them it seemed as though I always got my way. The important thing

to remember in our home was, "take care of my baby" (me), says

mom. Or get your tail beat by mom and dad. Well, to be truthful about

it, if you based this assumption on the first nine years of my life it

could be viewed as accurate. I can count on one hand how many

whippings I received during those years, and tell you what they were

for. It had to be something just unacceptable in our home or it

frightened my parents to death:

I threatened to burn down our house. I changed the price on a pair

of shoes in Kmart and got caught. I was playing tug-a-war with the

boys in the neighborhood one hot summer afternoon and I put all the

boys on one side against me. I thought I would have more strength

and beat them if I put the rope in my mouth, the boys tried to talk me out of it, but I insisted that I would beat them. Once they started pulling the rope, they pulled my two front teeth out. I threw an ink pen at my sister, hitting her right below the opening of her eye, because she kept pushing me and accusing me of eating her piece of watermelon when I had not. The last whipping I remember was for telling mom I was going to the neighborhood store, but instead I walked down town and was gone for several hours. The whole family was in an uproar and out looking for my niece and me.

I have four sisters, one brother, two half sisters and two half brothers, they all looked after me, and nobody better not mess with me. "Cause it would be going on," all I had to do was say the word. Shod, a beat down was nothing for them, but it's my good pleasure to do, to who ever, when ever, if I said the word.

Being tough or considered bad was the atmosphere in our home, an eye for an eye, tooth for a tooth, and fighting fire with fire was the mannerism of our spirits. Feeling bad about want you said or did, yeah right, you'll never know it. In fact, my parents quarreled and brawled all the time, it seemed to not bother me too much, but when it became extreme I never knew what to make of it.

3

A typical weekend in our home consisted of our immediate family, and my oldest half brother and his wife would come over. There would be fish frying, drinking, loud talking and cursing. "Girl go fix me a drink", I was obedient, fixing drinks and fetching beers, oftentimes I would fix myself one on the side. Returning to my room to play with my dolls and listen to music. The next thing I knew there would be commotion, and confrontation in the midst of our home. This lifestyle was just our way of life, I couldn't change it, it became apart of who I thought I was.

I am not trying to give or leave the impression only bad things occurred in our home. Sometimes we did enjoy one another. On Holidays like, Thanksgiving, Christmas, or maybe birthdays we would set around the table laughing and talking about the crazy things that we quarreled and brawled about. Yet and still when you are going through these incidents it truly wasn't funny. My parents took us on many camping trips, outings, and vacations. However the overwhelming fact remained the unstable behavior among my parents did not cease, while our sibling rivalries grew worse.

In addition to the topsy-turvy events which took place in our home I recall during elementary school I struggled in my classes, learning just came hard. I was put in a special reading class to help me read at the correct level. I would come home from school really excited about learning, wanting my parents to help me read the books I needed for school. As I set at the dining room table on the verge of crying, wanting so badly for someone to show interest in my lesson, but they were always preoccupied. No one asked or even seemed to be interested in helping me. I just knew I had better pass to the next grade level; **"so giving up was not an option."** This preoccupied state of mind, only concerned about one's self was the heart breaking reality of our home. I was like the little baby lamb that hung around; everyone was waiting on to grow up.

Phrases like, "I love you, and I'm concerned about you," were never openly expressed in our home. We knew we were loved as long as there was food on the table, a clean place for us to lay our heads, clothes were on our back, and we had shoes on our feet. What more could one ask for?

By the time I was ten years old I began to pride my life after learning from my sibling's mistakes. I would set and listen to my sisters conversations and say within myself, "I'm not going to let that happen to me, I'll make sure not to say that to mom or dad, or I'll never do that", and I didn't. I was one who could hear a conversation, taking in everything, with thoughtful attention, use their experiences, and learn from it as if I actually lived it. I would even socialize with my friends about it, teaching them as if I was an adult. Most people would say I was very mature for my age, because I knew a little bit about everything. I listened and for one purpose, to gain knowledge and understanding so that I could escape as many harmful situations as possible throughout my life.

The mistakes I made where not because I wasn't listening they were because I thought I knew all the mature and correct vindication's and didn't. I praise God that those mistakes are what have brought me to where I am today. In the position to help young people from all walks of life, by being a living example of what a difference the presence of God makes in a young person's life.

It does not matter what race you are, nor the color of your skin, if you are rich or even if you are poor. Satan has no preference; his spirit goes throughout the earth seeking, that which he can devour. Scripture leaves reference that his main objective is to "Kill" confidence, "Steal" peace and joy, and "Destroy" innocence, unity, and growth. Therefore, putting you spiritually in a position set for Hell. Satan targets the youth because they are young, very strong, and full of enthusiasm, that intense and eager interest in acquiring knowledge.

St John 10:10

10   The thief cometh not, but for to steal, and to kill, and to destroy: I am come that they might have life, and that they might have it more abundantly.

I Peter 5:8

8   Be sober, be vigilant; because your adversary the devil, as a roaring lion, walketh about, seeking whom he may devour:

The Lord gives us precise instructions that children should be taught concerning Him, so that they may learn to call upon Him, putting all trust and confidence in Him from their youth, to overcome the snares of Satan, and obtain eternal life. When a child's growth is directed and nourished in the inherent character of God through correction with beneficial purposes, over time this child will yield

bringing forth results (fruit) for carrying on this process.

"Train up a child in the way he should go: and when

he is old he will not depart from it."

Proverbs 22:6

"Children, obey your parent in the Lord: for this is

right, Honor thy Father and Mother; which is the first

commandment with promise; That it may be well with

thee and thou mayest live long on the earth. And, ye

fathers, provoke not your children to wrath: but

bring them up in the nurture and

admonition of the Lord."

Ephesians 6:1-4

Family Structure

In our home church on Sunday, that was good enough. I believe we attended every Baptist church in our community and never became faithful steady members at neither. I would hear occasional talk about getting baptized. More emphasis was placed on "Baptism" than on the development of a relationship through salvation with Christ. The consequential significance of this spiritual bonding with Christ was never discussed in my childhood home. Nevertheless, some how, some way, I knew there was a God out there. I prayed every night, not really knowing all the words to the Lord's prayer. Night after night, week after week, month after month, year in and year out I continued to pray. I just knew within my heart, mind, and soul that God heard my supplications.

Baptized three times seeking someone, something, in a maze of life uncertain of what was actually taking place spiritually and naturally in my life. Under the impression that once I had been baptized; if I were to die I would go to heaven. Baptism was suppose to be the key to my entire spiritual need. Yet, having done so time and time again, I was still hungry, very thirsty, and seeking a hidden answer to this longing thirst within me.

This is the way I would describe what happened to me through my eyes; the picture which comes to mind, is of a child born into a seemingly healthy family. This child's parents have become stagnant and are unable to provide adequate nourishing care for their child. Over time the child swiftly becomes malnourished due to lack of nutritious substance. It is an inevitable factor that if this child doesn't eat she shall perish. So as a means of survival she takes it upon herself to find care by testing and trying everything, nutritious or not that would satisfy that hunger aching pain within her stomach.

The nutritious substance symbolizes "Spiritual Guidance" in the word of God, and hunger represents the "Spiritual Void" in every human beings life and heart, once they are born into this world. This nurturing feeling of love, joy, peace, and acceptance only comes through the acceptance of God's son, Jesus Christ.

We were created to serve him.

"Except the LORD build the house, they labour in vain that build it: except the LORD keep the city, the watchman waketh but in vain. It is vain for you to rise up early, to sit up late, to eat the bread of sorrows: for so he giveth his beloved sleep. Lo, children are an heritage of the LORD: and the fruit of the womb is his reward. As arrows are in the hand of a mighty man; so are children of the youth. Happy is the man that hath his quiver full of them: they shall not be ashamed, but they shall speak with the enemies in the gate" (Psalm 127:1-5).

Chapter Two

Amazing Grace

I tried to put away those rough ways, now during my home life away from school and friends a lot of my time was spent singing in my bedroom. I played the trombone in the school band; music and singing were the love of my life. I would literally spend hours singing and rehearsing for pass-time or upcoming talent shows. When I was sad and feeling low, I would sing to myself because I had no other place to go. Music was my way of escape.

Lost and blind I was introduced to the Lord at ten years old, fifth grade. My grade school teacher, Ms. Saving Grace invited other students and myself to her church. I will never forget; it was an old dingy church house, which had an unpleasant stench called, Little Emmanuel Temple. Born again, the teachings begin to capture and relieve my spiritual hunger, and a relinquishing sense of belonging to someone was overwhelming, (Your first encounter with the "ALMIGHTY GOD" should make all the difference in your life). When I accepted His son as my Lord and Savior things changed for me, I began to experience another view of life.

Romans 10:9-10

9   That if thou shalt confess with thy mouth the Lord Jesus, and shalt believe in thine heart that God hath raised him from the dead, thou shalt be saved.

10   For with the heart man believeth unto righteousness; and with the mouth confession is made unto salvation.

That fighting mentality and unconsciousness of what I had done, or no remorse for the words I had said, went away. I became conscious of my errors. Finally I had accomplished something genuine, pure, and complete, full of love beyond compare.

II Corinthians 5:17, 18

17   Therefore if any man be in Christ, he is a new creature: old things are passed away; behold, all things are become new.

18   And all things are of God, who hath reconciled us to himself by Jesus Christ, and hath given to us the ministry of reconciliation.

[The world we live in has been reconciled unto God, he has given us all we need to overcome. Scripture teaches us that those who die in rejection of God's reconciling sacrifice (Jesus), have no further expectation except His wrath to come.]

I was on my way to heaven feeling the greatest, since I had found Jesus. I attended Sunday school, morning worship, midweek and tarrying services forming an inseparable spiritual bond with my Lord and Savior Jesus Christ. The things Ms. Saving Grace taught us that stuck with me even until now were, read your bible to learn God, pray every morning before going out, pray every night before going to bed, have faith in God, and most of all, Psalms the twenty third chapter. I memorized this scripture in my youth and hold it close to my heart.

Psalm 23   A Psalm of David

(A man after Gods heart)

1   The Lord is my shepherd; I shall not want.

2   He maketh me to lie down in green pastures: he leadeth me beside the still waters.

3   He restoreth my soul: he leadeth me in the paths of righteousness for his name's sake.

4   Yea, though I walk through the valley of the shadow of death, I will fear no evil: for thou art with me; thy rod and thy staff they comfort me.

5   Thou preparest a table before me in the presence of mine enemies: thou anointest my head with oil; my cup runneth over.

6   Surely goodness and mercy shall follow me all the days of my life: and I will dwell in the house of the LORD for ever.

Now that I had been redeemed, my life had never been better. I started receiving better grades in school and became an honor roll student. I went from fourth grade hardly able to read at the correct level, on to the fifth grade, accepted the Lord in my heart, to receiving A's and B's in all my classes. I was altogether a better child and I really didn't understand the fullness of it. However, I just felt something remarkable had happened within me, I felt better about myself, and encouraged about wanting better for my life. Things were going wonderful for me; I was considered one of the most popular students in my class, and attractive. I thought I had God and the World too, failing to realize my spiritual life would not and could not compare to my life in this World.

*"As it is written, I have made thee a father of many nations, before him whom he believed, even God, who quickenth the dead, and **calleth those things which be not as though they were**. Who against hope believed in hope, that he might become the father of many nations, according to that which was spoken, So shall thy seed be"* (Romans 4: 17– 18).

One cold winter night as Ms. Saving Grace dropped us off after church, we were all kind of complaining because her van was very cold, and it didn't have heat. Our hands, legs, feet, and toes were like ice sickles. As we continued to laugh and talk I remember her saying in a very direct, matter-of-fact manner, "Don't you all worry about it, God is going to bless us with a brand new van, which has heat. Just keep praying and believing in God."

We all just looked at one another and said, "We hope it's soon, like real soon!" Well it was approximately three years later; I no longer attended Ms. Saving Grace's church. I was walking home one

17

day from a friend's house, and decided to take the short cut through the alley. As I walked I saw this big maroon van backing out of the driveway, when it started moving toward me I recognized Ms. Saving Grace was driving. Immediately my mind went back to the cold ride home, that winter night, and what she told us. I felt I had to flag her down just to tell her I remembered what she told us and she was right, God had answered our prayer for a new van.

I don't know how, but from that moment on, the feeling I had was as if I had personally received the van myself. I had this huge smile on my face and the look of astonishment in my eyes. As I previously told you, I would listen to what other people said, to obtain knowledge, not knowing what Ms. Saving Grace spoke to us that night was a "seed" that began to flutter when I saw her blessing unfold before my eyes.

Chapter Three

Parental Trust Broken

When I was eleven years old my mother and father separated. Now this was a hard thing for me because I loved them both. Who do I believe? It's confusing to hear my mom say to my dad, "I know you have a woman you've been seeing on me." And hear him reply, "Woman you're crazy." But, not just that, he would also tell me, "Your mom is crazy I don't have another woman on the side." At eleven years old I was uncertain whom to believe? I never saw my father do anything; I just remember the phone would ring at all times of the day and night in our home, and it really bothered my mother. It never dawned on me this was part of dad's erroneous behavior.

Well after months of hearing my mother accuse my dad of being unfaithful and it was never proven; I eventually started to believe my dad, and I thought, "Maybe mom is crazy." A few more months passed and what was done in secret was brought out. I shall never forget the day, the memories are embedded in my mind. It was a hot summer morning during the month of July my father wasn't at home and hadn't been home all night. My mother received a phone call, someone told mom to go to a descreate location and there she would

find dad with his lover. My mom got dressed, now of course she was

hurt, but she was also very angry. I didn't know what to think, I just

said, "Oh no, no I can't believe this." I felt as if I was locked in a box

with no way to escape. I wanted to do something about this, and

couldn't. So I began to think, "How, how can I let this woman know

that she had ruined my family! Tearing my world apart, I knew my

parents marriage wasn't perfect but I loved them, I needed them, and I

needed them to be together for my sake." In a cry of despair, I

remembered mom said the last name of the woman who was with dad.

I got the phone book and found her number, but it turned out to be her

mother's number. I can't explain the mixture of emotions I felt. My

heart pounded, yet I had this boldness, and sense of I can fix this, I

thought in my mind. I dialed the number, an older lady answered the

phone, and I said, "Is Adultrina your daughter?" She answered,

"Yes", I said, "She has just been caught with my dad!" Then this fear

came over me and I hung up the phone. Reality set in, I thought I was

going to get in trouble for getting into my parents affairs.

When my mother return home that afternoon she was so hurt, I'm

telling you I felt her pain run all through me, I also felt angry and very sad toward my dad. I was afraid, wondering, "What's going to happen now? Mom where's dad, he's not with you?" Mom went directly to her room; the next thing I knew my mother was outside in our family motor home with a bat. Busting all the windows, cabinets, mirrors, and anything else that could be distorted, mom literally tore the inside of our motor home up. I would say for a minute there, "Mom had lost her mind!" She beat the inside of the vehicle until she became tired. I believe this was her way of releasing all of her hurt, anger, and pain. Well dad didn't come home after that incident, all that I could do was "Pray." The issue of how I felt or how I would deal with my pain was never discussed. My sisters never said anything nor did my brothers. My life was supposed to just go on, just as if my dad never existed. My life was truly changed, recalling moms exact words, "All men are alike, none of them are any good" hearing this time and time again. Those words were "seeds" planted in my mind (spirit) toward men. Mom had no idea that those words posed a potential threat in my life. Mom spoke these words in bitterness, anguish, and from past personal maltreated experiences. I received those words in detriment because of what my dad had done, and as veracity of all men.

22

{Now that I'm an adult I place neither fault nor blame on either of my parents, for I now realize and understand my mothers hurt. Furthermore, I count this entire episode as gain. I have learned now that I am a parent, parents must be certain that they are mindful of their present hurts, and the disappointments of their past when they make statements in the presence of their children.}

Just as GOD has given each man a measure of faith, the enemy (Satan) always seeks to counteract faith with seeds of distrust, skepticism, and antagonism. My challenge to you is, for you to train yourself to recognize his tactics naturally and spiritually.

Sibling Suicide

Adding to this entire situation, six months later one of my half brothers committed suicide. He hung himself.

One cold settle January night, not like most other nights since dad was not there, the house was quiet and peaceful. I was upstairs in my bedroom playing PAC-MAN on the Atari video game I had gotten for Christmas. It was getting late so, I kneeled on the side of my bed and started saying my prayers. Get this, in the midst of me praying to the Lord, I asked him to bless my family, allow mom and dad to get back together, and bless all my sisters and brothers. A few moments later, my prayer was interrupted by a shout from the bottom of the stairs. "Hey up there, yal brother just killed himself." I didn't and couldn't make sense of it all. I just knew I was very fond on this brother, I would say at that point he was my favorite. I used to spend a lot of time over at his home with him and his wife. He would take me riding in his car and allow me to work the gears. I just thought the world of the time I spent with him and his wife.

Receiving news of this magnitude was just unbearable, so I pretended it never happen. In other words I knew in reality the suicide happened, I just never accepted it. When my sister and I went to view his body at the funeral home, I had this feeling of great exasperation. My heart was pounding, I was breathing hard, and deeply, as I viewed my brother's lifeless body from a distance in that casket. I could not believe my eyes, my big brother was dead! It seemed like I was in a horror movie. The wake and funeral none of it, it all seemed like a nightmare.

Miraculously, due to this tragic event, my mom and dad did reconcile their differences and got back together. They were still quarreling, but that was okay with me, God answered my prayers, we were a family again. My dad was back home and that made me very happy. The Lord does work in mysterious ways.

Relief

If you have found that you have experienced any of these issues, or you are currently living in a home that is totally out of control. Maybe your situation is not exactly like mine was, or maybe it's better, or even worse. If you learn nothing else from my story, before you throw in the towel and give up at least give the LORD a chance. I'm telling you, your surrounding situation or circumstances may not change much. However if you give it to LORD, He will begin to make some changes within you. He will equip you naturally and spiritually for the struggle. I know "NO OTHER" who is able to do this. In other words the Lord takes potentially impossible, none repairable, life destroying situations, and make them work out for your good. Giving you peace in the midst of your disturbed or agitated circumstances. Right now I know you can agree that you have no peace of mind, when you are not sure what your future holds. The best advice I have to offer is, that you continue to pray, seeking the Lord with your whole heart, and putting all your trust and confidence in the one whom holds your future, "GOD."

Romans 8:28

28   And we know that all things work together for good to them that love GOD, to them who are the called according to his purpose.

Philippians 4:6,7

6   Be careful for nothing; but in every thing by prayer and supplication with thanksgiving let your requests be made known unto God.

7   And the peace of God which passeth all understanding, shall keep your hearts and minds through Christ Jesus.

PRESS, PRAY, AND PRAISE

A lot of times we question GOD asking him, "Why, Why must I feel the pain of a broken heart, of lose, discouragement, confusion, and anxiety?" I have come to this solution, calling it **"The Press to Pray to Praise"** our awesome GOD.

If your question is why?

Press, "Press and obtain Your Prize."

Pray, "Prayer ushers in the Presence of God."

Praise, "This Glorifies the Power of God."

Press, like the woman who had an issue of blood, twelve years and had depleted all her options for healing. She pressed her way through the crowd to touch Jesus (Matthew 9:20-22).

Your issue may not be like hers, however the answer is still the same. Do what ever it takes to press your way, for the Lord will see you just as He saw Zaccheus, who had climbed up a tree so that he could see Jesus as He passed by (Luke 19:1-6).

In your spirit you must do the same, having that same urgency.

Press to Pray to Praise Flow Chart

Press means push, go forward with a determined effort, forcing one's way.

Never Give Up!

Phil 3:14
I press toward the mark for the prize of the high calling of God in Christ Jesus.

Pray means make supplication or offer prayer to God.

Pray without ceasing.
I Th 5:17

If my people, which are called by my name, shall humble themselves, and pray, and seek my face, and turn from their wicked ways; then will I hear from heaven, and will forgive their sin, and will heal their land.
II Ch 7:14

Praise means to glorify God, expressing admiration and exalting in worship

Rejoice for-ever more.
I Th 5:16

By him therefore let us offer the sacrifice of praise to God continually, that is, the fruit of our lips, giving thanks to his name.   Heb 13:15

Chapter Four

Cross Roads

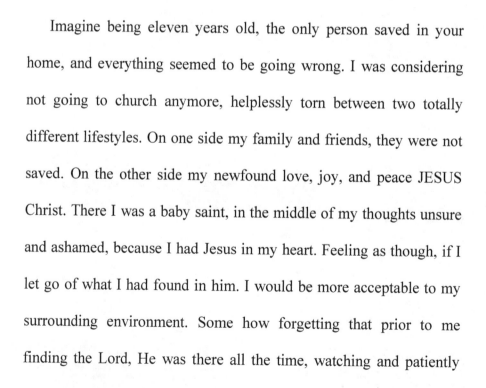

"Ye have not chosen me, but I have chosen you, and ordained you, that ye should go and bring forth fruit, and that your fruit should remain: that whatsoever ye shall ask of the father in my name, he my give it you" (St. John 15:16).

Imagine being eleven years old, the only person saved in your home, and everything seemed to be going wrong. I was considering not going to church anymore, helplessly torn between two totally different lifestyles. On one side my family and friends, they were not saved. On the other side my newfound love, joy, and peace JESUS Christ. There I was a baby saint, in the middle of my thoughts unsure and ashamed, because I had Jesus in my heart. Feeling as though, if I let go of what I had found in him. I would be more acceptable to my surrounding environment. Some how forgetting that prior to me finding the Lord, He was there all the time, watching and patiently waiting on me. That is why I longed for that void in my life to be filled. I was never really acceptable to the circumstances, and influences surrounding my life.

Nevertheless, I felt I had to choose the way I would travel, my family and friends or Jesus and salvation. One had to go, so due to my lack of maturity I chose to walk away from the LORD. I thought I had chosen on my own to walk with Christ anyway, but rather it was God who drew me to Him (St. John 15:16).

Once I made this decision, suddenly a depressing feeling of loss came over me. Troubled within myself, ignoring the warning of Holy Spirit within me. I managed to remain undistracted by the warring of my flesh against my spirit. I actually felt my soul cry out, as if I was trapped in a mirror, and when I saw myself I did not recognize who I was. I continued in my own way, unintentionally neglecting the kind of person I had become, because of God's "Saving Grace."

Not knowing the consequences of my decision. I was in a backsliden state, not sure exactly what I was doing. A lot of changes were taking place within me cognitively, physically, and emotionally.

I was beginning to put together the sexual things I saw at home on television, and I begin to listen to my girl friends tell their stories on how they were having sex, and how good and wonderful it was. I became curious of this sinful lifestyle. As a matter of fact I even became ashamed of being a virgin, which is something that every teenager should know to take pride in.

To me being one of the most popular girls in school, having plenty of friends, and being considered pretty were all I needed to fit in with the gang (World). Within one year the stress of peer pressure, popularity, the spirits of profanity, and lasciviousness crept in on me. {See, whenever you get to a point, once you are saved where you become confused about your salvation you are in a dangerous position. Why? Satan is trying to rob you of your inheritance. The only thing the World has to offer is the lust of the flesh and the pride of life. God always offers more}.

Ephesians 1:11 – 14

11   In whom also we have obtained an inheritance, being predestinated according to the purpose of him who worketh all things after the counsel of his own will:

12   That we should be to the praise of his glory, who first trusted in Christ.

13   In whom ye also trusted, after that ye heard the word of truth, the gospel of your salvation: in whom also, after that ye believed, ye were sealed with that Holy Spirit of promise,

14   Which is the earnest of our inheritance until the redemption of the purchased possession, unto the praise of his glory.

Chapter Five

Journey

> See clearly, the whole picture, please try not to blink, inhale take a breath if you need it, now exhale, and continue my journey.

One day I was standing in the hallway at school thinking, "The grass sure looks greener on the other side," I believed that was what I wanted for my life. Using profanity and exploring fun and crazy things to do, was the spark in the group of teenage girls I hung out with. Sure, I knew this was wrong, I just continued. Without even realizing what was happening to me, I found myself drifting further and further away from the new life I had found in Christ.

This happened because I chose to cut off all communications with the church and limited my relationship with the Lord. I knew I needed the Lord, I just didn't know how much! My pure, innocent, youthful life begins to take a drastic, dramatic, life changing turn for the worst:

Twelve years old (seventh grade), I was just informed of the arrival of a new male teacher who was approximately twenty-eight years old. My friend Manqué approaches me at the end of the school day.

"Have you seen the new teacher," she asked?

"NO," I replied.

"Come with me you've got to see him, he is so fine", said Manqué with excitement!

I followed her down the hall to gym where this teacher was. We looked through the small glass window of the gym door. When I saw this teacher for the first time I said to Manqué. "he looks all right, but he is not all that to me."

A few moments later this male teacher came out into the hallway. I proceeded walking down the hall toward the gym doors, to exit the school building. I noticed as I passed by him, that he looked kind of strange at me, maybe as if he were puzzled. I believed he wanted to introduce himself, but felt hesitant because I walked right by him just like I didn't see him. I imagined maybe he thought I was a teacher, because I was not acting gitty and silly in his presence, as my peers were. Through my eyes, he was just an older man, I did not know him, and I didn't find him to be, at first sight, simply gorgeous like all the others girls did.

Now, I didn't exactly look like a twelve-year-old girl either. Picture me, five feet seven inches, slim, shapely, black dress slacks, red blouse, black dress pumps, long curly black hair, red lip-gloss, and black eyeliner." Dressed and made up appearing to be a young woman. I caught this man's attention the very first time he laid his eyes on me.

{Pardon me, I really must tell you… it's just something, as I write and tell this story I can recall this experience as if it just happened yesterday.}

Unfortunately, none of my friends were bold enough to bother with this teacher because they were scared. Un-doubtingly, they knew I had no interest in him, and they also knew that I could and would accept a challenge. (The dare was that I walk pass this male teacher, appear to accidentally stop in front of him, look him in the eyes, and walk away.) So my peers pumped me up to act as such toward this twenty-eight year-old man. It was during a class break there he stood, five feet ten inches, muscular built, light complexion, with a presumptuous attitude. Outside his classroom door, leaning

37

backwards against the wall, just observing the students as they passed to their next class. All the young girls were giggling as they walked by him, because they thought he was the finest thing since "Prince." Well here I come dressed to kill walking pass him, head held high, moving my body maturely, with a straight face, glancing toward him briefly, blinking my eyes, and swaging my hair in such a way that it would definitely grasp his attention. Indeed it got his attention; he looked upon me with much pleasure as if I were desirable to him.

When I got back with my friends we were all laughing hysterically and they were telling me all about the way he looked at me. While the laughter, silliness, and excitement of this challenge was very hot and thrilling: It never really dawned on me, the situation I was creating for myself. Caught up in what you would call a childhood truth or dare challenge, which actually became a reality.

Satan had set me up. I was a sheep, which had gone astray and couldn't distinguish the many voices I was hearing. Once everything was said and done with my friends, I just couldn't get the way he looked at me off my mind. Not to mention the reinforced encouraging statements my friends made, "Girl he likes you", "Yeah, you two would make a good couple", "All the other girls like him too." It was just suppose to be showoff, fun, and games. I never expected to actually enjoy what I had done and the response I received for doing so.

It's now my eighth grade year, as the school year progresses I wanted to make sure I upheld my mature attitude at all times. I dressed well everyday, and whenever I was in the presence of this new teacher, I wanted to look attractive, sound intellectually developed, and impress him in doing so. Every encounter this man, (Lustful Deceit) and I had the more I desired his friendship and attention, not knowing his hidden true self sought to have me sexually. Being young, and not really knowing the possible consequences of seeking this type of attention from an adult male, I continued.

Again I emphasize, "with the encouragement of my peers" the situation was made more challenging. I felt like there was a point to be proven. What that point was, I didn't know.

{That is how most teenagers are, they can not explain why they do the things they do, they get caught up in the moment, their emotions, and what makes them feel happy and important to others for that

39

present time. Not taking in to consideration the potential danger or hazard they are creating for themselves}.

Back at home, things were still the same mom and dad were still quarreling. Mom worked hard all the time, dad didn't work because of an injury he received at work, which left him disabled. I continued to sing, quarrel with siblings, and listen to my sisters tell their stories on how their friends did this or how they did that. And how disappointed they were of how out of control our household was.

Sex and sexuality were certainly not a hush, hush subject in our home. It was a natural thing, mom said, "Once you get to be sixteen years old you will get on the birth control pill. So that if a situation arises you will be prepared for intercourse, just as long as you don't bring a baby home." The words that stuck in my memory with fear and trembling were, "Just as long as you don't bring a baby home!" My mom wasn't having that; she just didn't play.

Chapter Six

Deception of Innocence

This is my assumption of the situation, Mr. Lustful Deceit had a plan, and in his mind he had to figure out how he would get my attention, appear harmless, and gain my trust. Mr. Lustful Deceit would invite me to his classroom for study hall. We would talk about basketball because he was the boy's head coach and I played on the girl's team. He would make statements like, "Next year you'll become a full rounded person." I would say it took the rest of my seventh-grade year and part of my eighth-grade year for him to finally see that he had gained my trust. For Christmas, he gave me Gloria Vanderbilt Cologne and on my birthday he gave me money. Everytime he said something nice to me or gave me a gift I thought he just liked me. As a matter of fact, I would bring the gifts home and show my mom and she would say, "Oh that's nice. Not once did she inquire why, a male teacher would give gifts to a female student (minor). I believed my mom honestly thought there was nothing behind Mr. Lustful Deceit's kindness. So, neither did I, I knew I had like, a major crush on him but I never imagine it would go beyond that. Mr. Lustful Deceit liked me true enough, but he was just gaining my trust and testing the waters as he reeled me in. So that when he did touch me, I wouldn't tell. In my mind I was thinking we would just have a kiddy boyfriend girlfriend relationship. I even prayed to the LORD, I asked him to allow the relationship I had with Mr. Lustful Deceit to become closer. Before long this strange spirit arose in me and made me believe I was in love with this man. When the truth of the matter was, as it was only a simple childhood crush. For heavens sake, I was a twelve year-old virgin desiring to be close to a man who was willing and ready to abuse my innocence.

{Let me define a few things before we move on. The desire that attached itself to my spirit is called LUST. It began as a childish wish, which grew rapidly into an intense longing. At twelve or thirteen years of age one is not able to identify this spiritual sexual deceiver.}

One day during school, I was making popcorn deliveries to the classrooms. When I delivered Mr. Lustful Deceits to him in the boy's locker room office. Out of nowhere he came close to me, put his arms around me, and with his hands grasped my behind, then he kissed me

43

for the first time. No I did not resist him, in my thirteen-year-old world that's what I thought our relationship would come to and that's it. Afterward Mr. Lustful Deceit asked me, "Are you sure you can handle all this," He was referring to handling him being a man (sexually). Well, I was in absolute shock at the fact we kissed, "like on cloud nine." Of course I was scared, but the excitement and thrill of what had just happened over ruled the fear. I failed to mention to him that I was a virgin and the most that I had ever done was kiss a boy.

A couple of days later the boys and girls basketball teams had away games. Once we returned to the school that evening after the game Mr. Lustful Deceit approached me and said, "Don't worry about calling your ride tonight, I'll drop you off", so, I didn't call my sister as usual to pick me up. After the other players and coaches were gone that's when he made his move. He advanced toward me, standing in front of me, as I stood on the stairs facing the gym doors in the dark. Mr. Lustful Deceit said, "Kiss me", he held me very close to him and kissed me. He then paced the hallway as if he was double-checking whether or not everyone was gone. But that wasn't it at all, he was thinking about what he should do next, and how he would accomplish it. Well a few moments later he said, "Come with me, lets go." I thought we were just going to get some of his things from the basement office and go out of the gym doors.

When we entered the boy's locker room Mr. Lustful Deceit took me into this dark room filled with floor mats, I could tell they were mats because I was standing on one. Once he closed the door, there was complete darkness, the only light I could see came through the crack under the door. Mr. Lustful Deceit began to touch me all over my body while he was kissing me. Then he pulled me down toward the floor, he said, "Are you sure you can handle me?" I responded, "Ahum," shaking in my skin, and thinking, "I don't know what I'm doing, where's my mom, I want my mom! I can't tell him to stop now; it's too late!" While this rush of thoughts was running through my mind, the next thing I remembered was lying on a cold mat on the floor. My jeans were off, Lustful Deceit was over me, I heard the sound of paper rattling, and then he tried to penetrate my vagina area and he felt the resistance, realizing at that moment I was a virgin. Mr. Lustful Deceit didn't stop, he forced himself upon me, I held in my cry of pain for fear of what may happen. I clenched my teeth in excruciating pain until he finished. I couldn't recall how long the act lasted, but I was glad and relieved it was over. We exited the school through the boy's locker room from the basement doors. He drove me home and dropped me off at the corner were I lived. Hardly able to walk normally I forced myself to bare the pain, I was still trying to prove to this man, that I was a woman and not a child. Not knowing he knew all along that I was a child and that he had just violated my body and had taken my innocence.

When I entered my house that night I went to the kitchen to let my mom know I was home. Then I went directly up the back stairs to the bathroom and bathed. I ran the water as hot as I could bare it hoping that it would soothe the throbbing pain I felt between my legs. Afterwards, I went to bed.

The next day when I got up the pain was still there. I bathed again, dressed, and went to school. When I arrived at school, I entered the gym doors. There stood Mr. Lustful Deceit with this happy but stern look on his face, he said, "Hi." I replied, "Hi", yet continuing to walk and look straight ahead. As the flow of students and I moved down the hallway, Victoria, one of my classmates approached me and said, "Girl you should have seen how Mr. Lustful Deceit was staring at your body from head to toe when you walked by him." Continuing she said, "I also had a weird dream last night about you and Mr. Lustful Deceit, I dreamed that you and him were together last night and he had relations with you." But before she could finish I inadvertently interrupted her by saying, "Girl yeah right, I know that was a dream." Then I walked away kind of stunned at her words, pondering, "How could she know that?"

Well this was the first warning sign from the Lord to let me know he saw what happened, but I was too deaf to hear his voice and too blind to even see his hands reaching out to me, for I was in great danger.

Mya, another friend of mine approached me after lunch in the girls bathroom the same day and stated, "I heard from one of the janitors that he saw you and Mr. Lustful Deceit late last night when you went into the boys locker room, what happened, Mya asked?" I again blew off her statement and questions by saying, "I really don't think he saw anything, Mr. Lustful Deceit just gave me a ride home and that was it."

How ironic, I found myself defending Mr. Lustful Deceits and my innocence. The bazaar thing about it was, I wasn't really worried or anything about Mr. Frazer the janitor telling anyone, because he was guilty of the same thing himself. He was molesting the girl who just told me what he said. I knew that because Mya would tell me of their encounters.

Devices of Error

During our eighth-grade graduation party my friends had started using marijuana just for fun in celebration of our accomplishment. I also tried it for the first time, I didn't choose to use it because it was the cool thing to do. I knew it was a drug, and that it could cause damage to the cells in my brain, and it was not the will of God for my life. I thought about it, but it really didn't matter. It was summer break and I thought for sure that I would never hear from Lustful Deceit again. I earnestly sought relief from this pain, I felt deep within my heart for him.

When I tried marijuana for the first time it had absolutely no effect on me, I stayed the same and that heart felt pain still remained.

I was a little disappointed because I had thought this would take my pain away, at least for a few hours.

I recall explicitly the summer after eighth-grade graduations, my parents were taking a "Lady" friend of theirs to Birmingham Alabama to visit her mother. There was Ms. Lady, Mom, Dad, two teenage girls named, May, and Fay, and of course myself who were going. Birmingham was their home town, so they knew where all the college parties and night clubs were etc…."The live places to hang out."

From the very beginning my main purpose for going was to have fun, and as much as possible at that. I thought I could replace that inter heartache with partying and drinking. While we were there one of May's and Fay's cousins came and picked us up to go out to this club. When we arrived at the club called, "The Horse Shoe" I walked right in with no questions asked. Boy! This was extremely exciting for me (Remember I'm fourteen years old but I looked older). The atmosphere was off the hook. I ordered myself a drink and several men approached me asking to dance. Of course I declined, because I knew I was out of place. First off, if my mother knew where I was she would have killed me, I knew I was playing with fire. I'm talking straight up on the devils' turf, like in his back yard.

49

Unknown to us at the time, there was this man sitting in the distance watching us. As the night drew on he decided to approach us, as he passed our table he placed a marijuana cigarette on our table by my glass and kept walking. We thought he had done us a favor, so I put it in my bag for later. After leaving the club we went over to May's cousin's house, he was a young man in his early twenties. Fay and me couldn't wait, as soon as we got inside, we fired up the marijuana cigarette (joint) and shared it.

During the car ride home to Ms. Ladies mothers house, Fay and I both started feeling kind of funny, I was jittery and tingling, I began to feel out of my mind, like in the twilight zone. I couldn't distinguish if I was coming or going. I recall we all were behaving strangely. I thought to myself, "That man gave us a lace marijuana cigarette. That's why he gave it to us freely, he hoped we would smoke it while we were at the club then he would be able to have his way. Thank God for his grace, because I thought I was going to die, either from this drug, or from my mother murdering me when she found out, because we were acting real loud and crazy. As I laid in the bed that night I began to pray, "Lord God in heaven Help Me! Please forgive me for what I have done, and deliver me from this feeling, and behavior. Lord if you do, I'll never touch another marijuana cigarette again." God came through for me and I did not die, neither was I sick the next morning.

I'm sharing this because a lot of teenagers fall victim to situations such as this. Some escaped the hook but others don't, I was just blessed to. Never take drugs from a stranger or a so-called friend. Drugs are not a game they are sin and lead to destruction, sickness, and death. Drugs have no respect of person and they do not recognize age. They can not make things better for you; they only cause more problems. Most of all never trust your life to anyone; life is real, and a very precious gift from God. I realized that during my experience with marijuana, for "he" was truly not my friend!

Continue the Journey

Well the sexual encounters between Mr. Lustful Deceit and myself continued through out the remainder of my eighth-grade year and even well into my freshman year in high school. I found myself entangled in this behavior, desiring to have relations with this man and didn't understand why. Lying to my parents about where I was going, when I was really sneaking to be with Mr. Lustful Deceit. He would rent hotel rooms so that I could come see him and once he got his apartment in the city I lived in, he would pick me up and we would go to his place.

You want to talk scary and dangerous, I had put myself in situations that possibly could have gotten me kidnapped, rapped or even killed by someone other than him. I waited on dark corners and behind big bushes in my neighborhood for Mr. Lustful Deceit to pick me up. It wasn't like we were friends and talked about things that we had in common. We were from two different generations, the only purpose I served for him was his sexual lust filled fantasies and perverted desires in having intercourse with a child.

Caught up in a world of uncertainties an emotional roller coaster. I anticipated one day Mr. Lustful Deceit would be able to meet my family and we would get married. Right, this was the furthest thought in his mind. Once he got a live in girl friend he told me he didn't want me calling his house anymore, it was over between us. That's just how it was, I was totally devastated. The question was where and who do I run to? I couldn't talk to my mom, look to sisters for advice, or even friends to comfort me. I was on my own to battle this hurt. It was like one I had never felt before. When Mr. Lustful Deceit told me this I was talking to him on a pay phone at school. As I walked home that day I talked to myself saying, "What's wrong with me? I knew I was younger than he was, but I thought I had proven to him I was just as able to fulfill his needs as someone of his age." I thought if I allowed him to have my body I was someone special, and he thought so to. I walked, cried, and mumbled my thoughts aloud saying, "This will never happen to me again." I thought life just didn't seem the same and I didn't have any close friends at this point. Things at home were still the same. I found myself once again desiring to hear that little voice that I would hear that guided me, but He was no longer present.

Imagine me fourteen years old a backslider and didn't even know it, in search again of relief, suffering a pain most women twice my age would be experiencing. Because the person I had replaced God with had just pushed me away.

Well I found myself looking to the Lord through gospel music and secular music trying to subdue the hurt in my heart. I kept moving and buried this hurtful disappointment, counting it as a lesson learned.

I started attending a new church. It was one that my mother had chosen and was now making one of my sisters and me attend. It was a sanctified holiness church, it was there that I repented and asked for forgiveness for my sins and asked that Lord to lead and guide me once again. The Lord had forgiven me but I still found myself carrying a yoke, which kept me, bound. This condition of being under another's power or control was warring within my flesh. I was no longer seeing Mr. Lustful Deceit, yet my flesh still desired him. I sought relief from this desire. The need for deliverance was an inevitable necessity. Unfortunately, it didn't come soon enough. See the thing was, I had a broken heart, which made me susceptible to the opposing lustful force that lied within me.

Every now and then Mr. Lustful Deceit would call me and we would get together for relation purposes only. I knew about his live in girl friend but that didn't matter. Afterward, I always found myself convicted repenting asking the Lord to give me yet another chance. Mr. Lustful Deceit continued to come and go in and out of my life for approximately one more year. Until the unthinkable happened!

This is what happened, Mr. Lustful Deceit called me one night, he said, "What will you be doing later?" I replied, "Oh nothing." He said "Well can I pick you up later and we go for a ride?" I said, "Sure" Later that evening he picked me up at the corner. We drove out toward the country where there were no streetlights. He pulled to the side of the road. Then he started to touch and fill all over me as usual when we would get together. However, on this night it was different. I realized I didn't have those same feelings I used to have for him. We had not seen each other in months so I didn't expect that he would try anything like this in his car. Well I was wrong, thinking that we were just going to take a ride. I was actually trying to live saved and resist that desire in my flesh, but because I chose to put myself in this situation, before I knew it one thing lead to the next and when it was over he took me home. I knew it would be days possibly before I would hear from him again.

One month later, it was one-month before my fifteenth birthday, and I had missed my menstruation for the first time. Regretfully, finding out that I was pregnant by Mr. Lustful Deceit. The joy of turning fifteenth was evasive, instead great sorrow and fear compassed me about imprisoning my spirit. Fear of what my mom was going to do to me when she found out was breath taking. All I could hear in my thoughts was her voice saying, "You better not bring a baby home!" I prayed and I prayed, "Lord please don't let this be true. I can't be pregnant," but the truth was I reaped what I had sown through the manipulate ways of Lustful Deceit, and my disobedience to the word and voice of God.

A CRY FOR HELP

In despair I called one of my siblings and told of my dilemma. The disbelief that was conveyed was heart breaking, "Oh No, this can't be!" We have to do something about this. In other words, I was not having a baby at fifteen years old. I was told not to tell a soul of this incident. Then three weeks later I was taken to an abortion clinic in Chicago. This clinic was filled with young girls and women (Black, White, Hispanic, Asian, and others) preparing to have abortions. I will never forget that experience. When we arrived I had to fill out a medical application, and then therapists counseled me. They told me that the procedure, which was chosen for me, was the most expensive and safest procedure. They asked if I had ever done this before, and if I knew what the procedure was? At no point was I asked if I was sure

I wanted to do this, because I guess I wouldn't have been there if that was the case. I thought, "I just want this problem to be gone and gone fast."

They explained that I would be given anesthesia to put me to sleep and oxygen while they preformed the procedure, which would last approximately twenty minutes. Once it was over I would be taken to the recovery area for one hour. It was just that simple they assured me, all your troubles will be over. I went and dressed for the surgery. When I entered the room and laid on the table they administered the anesthesia to me and placed the oxygen mask over my face. How did I know that if I was asleep? Well, I wasn't, my body was asleep but my mind was still awake so I could hear and feel what was going on around me. Next I heard the suction machine come on which sounded like a vacuum. All of sudden I wanted to changed my mind, but it was too late. The machine was going the doctor and nurse were talking. I started panicking on the inside, I was saying, "No, no I want my baby!" I tried to close my legs, move my arms, and lift my body up off the table, but I couldn't. I kept fighting and it was to no avail, I thought I was dying, the oxygen mask seemed to be suffocating me.

Then the machine went off and I heard the doctor say, "Awake her." The nurse put this liquid on a cotton ball and put it under my noise as she tried to wake me up. I kept going in and out of consciousness, when they asked me to stand so that I could get into the wheel chair, I couldn't because I was too weak and would fall down, they tried to help me but I was still sliding down. So they had to pick me up and put me in the wheel chair. At this point, tears were rolling down my face like tidal waves; I started vomiting all over the floor. They gave root beer to help stop the vomiting. Once I was in recovery the nurse gave me these little white pills to help shrink my uterus back to it's normal size and stop the bleeding. Then and there I realized I had made an irreversible mistake. I allow someone to kill my baby, and I could have even been killed myself without considering the consequences of this action. Traumatized but the whole incident I gained the strength to pull myself together and walk out or there. My sibling was in the waiting area when I returned. I was asked, "Are you okay?" I said, "Yes I'm fine", and we walked out of the clinic.

When I was dropped off at home, I went straight to my bedroom and fell asleep. During the night I woke up, I got on my knees in my bed, and cried out to the Lord asking him to forgive me for what I had done. For some reason I felt in my heart that he had forgiven me too, yet I couldn't even forgive myself. I blamed myself for the whole thing I thought I should have been smarter than that. At no time did I stop and say, "look Mr. Lustful Deceit did this to me, I'm the child and he's the adult."

{Typically, that's how it goes most of the time with victims of molestation and other sexual abuse cases. The victim feels that it is their entire fault and there should have been something they (the victim) could have done to perhaps change the outcome.}

The next morning when I got out of bed my whole body was sore, like I had been squeezed through a ringer, tossed and thrown. I'm telling you every muscle in my neck, arms, abdomen, and legs were sore. At first I couldn't figure out why, but later it came to me it was due to me trying to fight through the anesthesia during the abortion. My chest felt like it had weights on it and my heart had shriveled up and sunk deep within. Forcing myself to go on, I refused to stay home from school that day, because of the fear of being alone with my conscious. I lost all focus on my education and the only thought in my mind was, "I want my baby back!" I was full of guilt, and despair, I felt like I had to fix what I done wrong. From that moment on my mental and emotional stability began to diminish. I was falling apart psychologically, saying to myself, "You're a murderer, thou shall not kill, that's one of the Ten Commandments, you killed!" I had nightmares and everytime I saw a commercial or heard someone talk about a baby I would just crumble on the inside. My competence in using the camouflage technique to hide my heartache was swiftly fading. As I sat in my room a few days later thinking everything over and crying, I just started going crazy, raging totally out of control, swinging my arms, jumping around out of anxiety and guilt. I pulled everything off my walls, knocked everything off the dressers, throwing, hitting myself, and into the air, I pulled everything insight, throwing it to the floor, and uttering from deep within, almost like a groan, "I want my baby back, I want my baby back!" I continued until I was exhausted. I did this knowing in actuality, "the damage was already done", now it is time for me to move on, but I couldn't.

In the midst of all the commotion I made that afternoon, I believe my brother heard me in my bedroom. A few hours later He said, "Come here Boo, what's going on with you? You can talk to me, I know something is wrong with, you're not acting like yourself. You can't fool me." (See my brother started calling me 'schizo' because of the changes in my attitude, but he and I would just laugh about it). Well I looked him directly in his eyes and said, "I had an abortion", he said with much concern, "Oh no, come here," and he grabbed me and held me real tight and talked to me. As he held me and talked, I just cried as a means of release of this great mental anguish from my heart.

{I know now that I'm an adult, that this was the intervening power, everlasting mercy, and unfailing grace of my GOD. He opened my brothers' eyes to see that I was hurting and used him to minister unto me that day. I honestly believe that if that wouldn't have taken place, I possibly would have considered harming myself.}

Lust and Her Destructive Power

Lust is deceitful and is also translated to mean, "delight in desires for the things of the world (carnality), passionate desire as well as sexual desire."

These scripture expound on what lust is, her purpose, what she will cause if you yield to her, and how she will cause you to become unproductive in the word of God, which is detrimental during your spiritual journey with Christ.

Then verse 17 tells you the rewards of walking in unrighteousness and in walking upright before God in holiness.

I John 2:15,16,17

15   Love not the world, neither the things that are in the world. If any man love the world, the Love of the Father is no in him.

16   For all that is in the world, the lust of the flesh, and the lust of the eyes, and the pride of life, is not of the Father, but is of the world.

17   And the world passeth away, and the lust there of: **but he that doeth the will of God abideth forever**.

The after effects of lust on the word of GOD:

Matthew 4:18,19

18   And these are they, which are sown among thorns; such as hear the word,

19   And the cares of this world, and the deceitfulness of riches, and the lusts of other things entering in, choke the word, and it becometh unfruitful.

The consequence of carnal thinking:

Romans 8:5-8

5   For they that are after the flesh do mind the things of the flesh; but they that are after the Spirit, the things of the Spirit.

6   For to be carnally minded is death: but to be spiritually minded is life and peace.

7   Because the carnal mind is enmity against God: for it is not subject to the law of God, neither indeed can be.

8   So then they that are in the flesh cannot please God.

Chapter Seven

The Call

Watch, continue, and endure... MY JOURNEY;

The Vision

It was my sixteenth birthday; I was very excited because I could officially start courting. In our house the rule was you couldn't go out on dates, talk on the phone to boys, and no male friends could come over to see you until you became sixteen. Why, my mom was not strict on some of my sisters, and strict on the other ones and myself, I never knew. Due to this rule I had been sneaking out to be with this young man for almost six months. So it really meant a lot to me that my parents would finally get to meet him. I had it all planned out Fornication was to pick me up at six o'clock p.m. I would introduce him to my parents then we would go out for a movie and pizza. Well Fornication didn't show up that night. I waited, and waited, and waited. I even spoke to him earlier that evening and he said he would be at my house as planed. Six o'clock p.m. came and went, seven, eight, and nine o'clock p.m. even passed, no Fornication. My feelings of satisfaction, completeness, and excitement quickly turn to disconsolation and perplexity. I couldn't fathom why Fornication would lie to me and cause my heart to ache as if it were melting away.

Maybe the stand up wouldn't have been so bad if I wasn't so focused on having a serious relationship replace the one-sided one I had with Mr. Lustful Deceit.

Gods Call

Setting in my room in front of the mirror, debilitated in unbelief and sorrow, I immediately resented myself. Staring deep into my own eyes, I thought to myself, "What's wrong with you? Why do you keep making the same mistakes?" I begin saying out loud. "You are so stupid! You are so stupid! Why am I not good enough?" Then with my teeth gritted, and my lips tightened, I started slapping and hitting myself in the face over and over again, lacking the ability to control my emotions, I continued. While I was in the very act I heard a voice sound out from up above my head, yet into my ears saying, "What you are going through, will help others." Astonished I looked up to see who or from whence this voice had come. Conceiving mentally it was the voice of the Lord speaking to me. He again said, "What you are going through, will help others." When I lifted up my head and eyes to the ceiling, for a brief moment the Lord open my spiritual eyes, as if I were in a trance I beheld a glimpse of my future. What I saw in the vision was, myself on a stage, standing behind a podium before a large multitude of young people, like in a school auditorium speaking, I thought. The Lord only allowed me to see it momentarily, and I was not permitted to hear what I was saying. Then just as this vision appeared in a cloud it closed and vanished away. I stopped crying and didn't hit myself anymore. The Lord helped me to regain composer of myself, I believe I may have been in shock. The whole experience was indescribable, yet it made a profound spiritual impact in my life. I felt, I was not alone, for the Lord was right there carrying me.

Test

A few days later Fornication called me, and of course I forgave him, when I should have not continued on with that fornication based relationship. I did like most teenage girls do, I allowed him to give me some old lame excuse for him not coming over to meet my parents.

I continued to go to church and listen to sermon after sermon, I began to say, "I know this lifestyle is not healthy and it is not the will of God that I continue on this way." I had my Pastor pray for me, he prayed that I would be delivered from the wounds of my past broken heart. After this prayer that heavy weight I felt on my heart every morning, went away.

I cut myself away from talking and seeing Fornication. Not that he cared at this time, because he was involved with a girl who was the same age as him, twenty. A few months passed and I started dating other people, but nothing I considered serious. You would have thought that due to the length of time Fornication and I stopped talking I would have built up some type of resistance. Mistakenly I hadn't, due to lack of studying Gods word and steady communication with other saved teenagers. I drew very weak spiritually, and I let my natural guards down. I say this because I truly struggled with that fornicating demon. It convoked me into believing I still had to replace the child I had previously aborted and that molestation partner through the longing within my flesh.

One day Fornication called and I was actually happy to hear from him. We started talking on the phone again at his convenience. Before long we were talking almost every day and I found myself back entangled by his smooth talking and manipulative ways. This was especially critical and dangerous for me, because I saw what type of character Fornication possessed. He was just looking out for what he could get form me, which was to defile my body, the temple of the Holy Ghost.

After being delivered from his sexual holds on my heart, I allowed myself to become subject to them, "Lust and Fornication," once again. Instead of being subject first to what I knew God said in his word, the relationship I had with Jesus, my parents, my Pastor, and above all the voice of God that I would hear which warned me in the time of trouble. I was disobedient and this time the consequences were much worse.

I had graduated from high school, my junior year and enrolled at the Junior College as a Vocal Music Major, you see my dream was to be a vocal music teacher.

It was the hot month of August everyone was preparing for school, excited, and looking forward to obtaining a college education and a brighter future. Everything seemed to be working out for me, I was happy, however I just didn't seem to be myself. The end of the month approached I found out that I was pregnant again, and this time by Fornication. I again tried praying asking God, "Please don't let it be so." Nevertheless, it was a fact, I thought to myself, "Now I know there are many other young people out there having sex much more than I am, and I slipped up one time this month giving in to Fornication and look at what has happened!" I was scared but not like before because I was out of High School and I thought things were going to be different this time.

I informed Fornication of "our" pregnancy, thinking he was going to be supportive. Well, it seemed as though he was, for a while then he became just the opposite. He begin to ask questions like, "Are you sure the baby is mine? Or are you sure you've only been with me?" Knowing good and well the child was his and I hadn't been with anyone else but him. He even started playing games, like deliberately avoiding my phone calls, or having his mother, and brother say he wasn't home when I called. I put up with this for another two to three weeks. Then I called Fornication's house and spoke with his mother telling her the dilemma her son and I were in. Watch and listen to Ms. Pitiful (Fornication's mother) responses.

Ms. Pitiful answers the phone, "Hello." I said, Hi is Fornication home?" She replies, "No." I told her that I actually called to speak with her and wanted her to know that I was pregnant by your son, Fornication. I thought that maybe she would be able to talk to Fornication about this issue. Ms. Pitiful said in great amazement and fury, "You are what! How did "you" let this happen?" Then she said, "You know how males are." (I'm thinking by this time I am seventeen years old but Fornication is twenty). Totally dumb founded by her words, I wondered why is she fussing at me? Out of respect for her being Fornication's mother I just said, "Yes mam, then I hung up the phone."

{Let us face the fact girls, it is always expected or assumed that the female should be the wiser of the two, when it comes to this area of life. Unfortunately, this is a misconception, whenever there is an unborn child involved both partners (male and female) are responsible **not just the female.** In addition, if one of the partners is minor, the parents of that child are responsible, and if the other partner is of legal age, the proper authorities should be notified.}

I saw then that his mother could care less about her son, this unborn child, or me. I felt like if I didn't have the support of the baby's father nor his mother, then I would be on my own to care for this child. At no time did I consider what my parents would say, or even to confide in them. I automatically assumed all hell was going to break loose at my house if my parents found out.

So, I confided in a close friend of mine. I believed she was very upset with me and she showed me no empathy. She just said, "You do not want a baby! Not now anyway!" We made preparations for our trip to the abortion clinic in Chicago. The night before and even every night leading up to that day. I would Pray, "Lord please forgive me, allow your will to be done, bless me to make it through this." I was afraid of those clinics because of what they were and because of my previous experience. I just felt this time like I was going to die.

I broke my promise to God; I told him I was sorry for having the first abortion, now here I am again back in the same predicament on the verge of having another one and did.

That day I will never forget, I had no idea what I was about to undergo. We couldn't afford the type of abortion I had the first time, and we only had enough money for the cheapest. Which was the one where you are just given one shot of a local anesthetic somewhere near your pelvic area. My friend and I both thought this would be fine.

When I entered the clinic room I got up on the table, they gave me that shot. Then immediately started the procedure. The suction machine was going, the doctor inserted the suction tube into my vagina, and I felt them rip the baby from within me. It felt like a vault of lightening or electricity was inside of me. The pain was unbearably awful, like none I had ever felt or imagined. My body was jerking as the doctor continued to suction what was left from my uterus. When the procedure was over I went to the recovery room to lay down for a while, a nurse give me some little white pills to stop the bleeding. Afterward I was release to go home.

After I returned home from Chicago, I went directly to my bedroom and stayed for the remainder of the night. While I was in there I just prayed, I didn't know if God would listen to me, because I had done such a terrible thing and this was the second time. I could have chosen to have this child, whether or not the father or his mom would be supportive of us. I knew what was right, yet I had done wrong, why should God even care?

Based on facts I previously stated, I was guilty of disobedience to Gods word, lust, fornication, and murder. Notwithstanding, in my press for forgiveness:

I got down on my knees before the Lord and told him, "Lord, I'm sorry but you know all and you know my heart." "Lord please forgive me for I have sinned against you."

I go on to ask for myself, "Lord deliver me from this spirit of lust and fornication because I can not do it on my own, I've tried and I'm failing."

Then I said, "Lord if it is your will, please send me a husband, someone who's able to deal with me and someone who understands what I've been through, in Jesus name Amen."

I got up off my knees and put on a cassette tape, laid in my bed, and went to sleep trusting that the Lord would answer my prayer.

I was a music lover; R&B and Inspirational music always played a very important part in my life. No matter what type of music I chose to listen to I was always drawn to songs that reflected on the issues that were current going on in my life. As a teenager most of my present hope and future dreams were encouraged through the lyrics of a song. When I listened to music I actually felt every word.

I was the type of person who thrived on the lyrics of a song. To me lyrics are what make the music effective and they set the mood and atmosphere for the listener. I peculiarly found that inspirational music released peace within my mind and hope, the type of hopes I desperately sought to find. Inspirational music helped carry me through those lonely, rough, ridged, and unbearable times.

One of the songs that I found to be most vital during my journey was titled, **"Running Back To You"** recorded by a group called Commissioned, with Fred Hammond singing lead. Lord knows I thought this song was written just for me. Due to the complexity of circumstances going on in my life it was like the lyrics of this song expressed exactly what I had been experiencing in my walk with Christ. They spoke to God the words I could not find.

I always found myself running back to the Lord. I found him to be merciful, patient, and faithfully waiting for me to see all I needed was him. Although I had behaved inappropriately, God knowing all things, knew I was not going to make it on my own. Like, "The Prodigal Son" I would come running back home to him.

I recall while in high school and at church I sung this song on numerous occasions. It was like a testimonial song of my life. I remember my mother and I went out of town to visit relative in Southern Illinois, while we were there we went to church and I was asked to sing a solo. I sung "Running Back To You." My mom asked me afterwards, "Why did you chose to sing that song?" She added, "It was sad." I just looked at my mother, kind of laughed, and hunched my shoulders, not saying anything. (Well, mom if you are reading this book you know why now. And I don't mean that sarcastically. This is from my heart).

Chapter Eight

Self Expression

Deliverance Speaks

It may seem as though I am no ways near;

Yet, I am as close as your next breath is near.

If you draw nigh to God,

He will allow me to draw nigh to you.

Experience the moment,

take a simple breath, inhale and exhale.

My presence is so near,

cleanse your hands and purity your heart,

the LORD is faith and just who promised,

to cleanse us from all unrighteousness.

For after all the things that you have done wrong,

the LORD is still the only one who can forgive you and guide you

back to Him.

Hebrews 10:23

23   Let us hold fast the profession of our faith without wavering;

(for he is faithful that promised;)

I John 1:8,9

8   If we say that we have no sin, we deceive ourselves, and the truth is not in us.

9   If we confess our sins, he is faithful and just to forgive us our sins, and to cleanse us from all unrighteousness.

10   If we say that we have not sinned, we make him a liar, and his word is not in us.

Colossians 1:21,22, 23, 23

21   And you, that were sometimes alienated and enemies in your mind by wicked works, yet now hath he reconciled.

22   In the body of his flesh through death, to present you holy and unblameable and unreproveable in his sight:

23   If ye continue in the faith grounded and settled, and be not moved away form the hope of the gospel, which ye have heard, and which was preached to every creature which is under heaven;

Self Expression

I was what you would call the occasional fornicator. Meaning I only committed this act once or twice a month if that. I never intended on becoming pregnant nor having an abortion. I heard that pregnancy is a result of what happens when a male and a female fornicate (have premarital sexual intercourse). However, I have learned that this act only has to happen once and last one second, for pregnancy to occur.

Of course, I knew fornicating was a sin, however I couldn't resist the temptation. I didn't know how to, or were to begin on fighting this unclean spirit which lied deep within. Fornication had a strong hold on my life and I allowed it to through the manipulation of others and my lack of knowledge.

To me it seemed like most adults were silent concerning the major biblical facts on this issue. "If I am expected to make it, sit me down and explain the purposes of this behavior. I am a teenager I can't resist being left to wonder, speculation, and eventually engage in this act with out caution."

Gal 5:17   For the flesh luseth against the Spirit, and the Spirit against the flesh; and these are contrary the one to the other; so that ye cannot do the things that ye would.

I Thessalonians 4:3,4

3   For this is the will of God, even your sanctification, that ye should abstain from fornication:

4   That every one of you should know how to possess his vessel in sanctification and in honor;

Sex is an important natural fact of life, which was orchestrated by God so that men and women could be fruitful, multiply, and replenish the earth as husband and wife (Genesis 1:27, 28).

So there you have it, just knowing that fornication is wrong isn't good enough; you must practice living a clean life that's dedicated solely to God especially if you find yourself weak in this area. Don't allow your friends to tell share their sexual encounters with you. I know you're wondering why, because you are not doing anything but listening and there is no harm in listening. "Now that's where you are wrong," for their unclean words will take root in your spirit planting a seed of lust. If you continue to partake in those conversations (with your ears) it will destroy (teardown) the good knowledge you have been taught as a child of God.

Ephesians 4:29

29   Let no corrupt communication proceed out of your mouth, but that which is good to the use of edifying, that it may minister grace unto the hearers.

Ephesians 5:1, 3, 5, 6, 7

1   Be ye therefore followers of God, as dear children;

3   But fornication, and all uncleanness, or covetousness, let it not be once named among you, as becometh saints;

5   For this ye know, that no whoremonger, nor unclean person, nor covetous man, who is an idolater, hath any inheritance in the kingdom of Christ and of God.

6   Let no man deceive you with vain words: for because of these things cometh the wrath (anger) of GOD upon the children of disobedience.

7   Be not ye therefore partakers with them (separate yourself).

II Corinthians 6:14,17

14   Be ye not unequally yoked with unbelievers: for what fellowship hath righteousness with unrighteousness? and what communion hath light with darkness?

I Cor 15:33

33   Be not deceived: evil communications corrupt good manners.

Chapter Nine

Lesson Learned

It's approximately two months later, Friday October thirty-first, Halloween night. I was supposed to be in church that night. However, my friend Joy and I drove to the church, pulled into the church parking lot, and I parked. We were unsure on weather or not we wanted to stay or go hang out with some unsaved friends. We began to talk and reason with one another and we decided to leave. Instead of going on home we decided to go over to a male friends house. He had just gotten a new apartment and had invited a few people over to celebrate. When Joy and I arrived we sat and conversed with every one.

Meanwhile, my friend Bruce had previously introduced me to one of his friends "Death in Defeat." We had talked on the phone a few times, but had never really seen each other. This was the first time, "Death in Defeat" and I met face to face.

Death in Defeat and I found a place were we could talk privately. While we talked Death in Defeat put his arm around me, and later we begin to kiss, and kissing lead to us having what we called a one-night stand. Of course we used protection, so I thought I had no reason to worry about becoming pregnant this time. I really had no true feelings for Death in Defeat and what happened between us only happened because we both got caught up into the heat of the moment "Lust and Pleasure."

I don't know, I must have, for that period of time forgotten what I had promised God. "I'll be fine," I thought. I assumed, I could have sex the safe way, and get away with it, but instead it backfired on me.

I found myself one month later facing the same dilemma, "I was pregnant again." I told Death in Defeat and he said, "You know we can't have this child." I replied, "Why? Why not?" He says, "Because I'm in college, I have goals, and plans for my future, having a child right now is not part of my dream." "I don't want you to have my baby." "I'll pay for the abortion and everything, I don't care, I'm just not ready to be a father!" He went on to say, "Hey look, I'm not the man for you, I'm not ready to settle down and that's what it seems like you are looking for. I'm not him! Maybe you'll meet that someone, one day, and you'll have a family." You see money was not an option or problem for Death in Defeat because his family was pretty well off.

As he spoke, I sat there listening flabbergasted, I felt as though Satan himself was speaking to me, and now I was stuck between what you would "a rock and a hard place." I was being asked to do the very thing I just asked the Lord to forgive me for, just three months prior. I fought with myself over the decision, I thought I had no other alternative so I did as he wished.

I justified what we had done by saying and convincing myself, "I wasn't going to be no fool, he told me up front how he felt." Death in Defeat was not ready to be a father!

Guilt stricken, shame, broken, and feeling like the lowest thing that could walk this earth. Even the fear that I may never be able to have children entered into my spirit, due to the traumas I put my body through. To me, I had destroyed my children, which were a gift from God and my inheritance; my body because I allowed my fleshly desire to over rule my spiritual knowledge of God; and most importantly my relationship with God. I knew I was in trouble because I really didn't know what to do, or who to turn to.

Finally, I had learned my lesson and this was the last occurrence of this repetitive cycle of behavior. I felt like I had received the worse whipping of my life both naturally and spiritually. So I came totally clean with God at this time. I made up in my mind I could never go through another abortion as long as I lived. I would never let another male touch me until it was the husband that God gave me. As a matter of fact, I was so scared, worn, and tired I didn't even want to hear nor see the words "Abortion nor Fornication," or seem remotely interested a male friend for companionship.

It was at my lowest point when God was then able to speak to me and I was very eager to listen. He revealed to me that due to the short period of time in which I had the last two abortions, I was supposed to have died on that table during the last one.

He proceeded to show me how He protected me in the midst of it all. I began to reminisce the sequence of events of that day. When I entered the clinic room and laid on the table, three nurses or what I thought to be nurses, and one doctor entered behind me. One of nurses took my arm, told me to relax, and she started talking to me as she inserted the needle into my arm. I recall the other two nurses just stood around me. I found that to be very comforting.

When the abortion was completed I was awakened and there stood those same three nurses by my side. I didn't know what to make of it. I had no recollection of what happen once I fell asleep. I did kind of wonder and found it very strange that they seemed to care about me. I thought to myself, "When I went through this the other two times there was one doctor and one nurse." I suspected they were there to make sure everything went smooth. But never in my wildest dreams would I have ever imaged God had place them there to protect me, yet he had. Especially when I was doing something so wrong.

My ways are not His ways neither are my thoughts like His, for there is none that is like Him.

Song of Zion

During this particular time in my life I thanked God for the song titled, "You Bring Out The Best In Me" by Vanessa Bell Armstrong. Those of you who don't know this song really won't relate to what I mean when I say, "The Lord knew I would need this song when he gave it to Vanessa." You see I took the lyrics to this song personally. Once I truly realized I couldn't make it on my own, and I had made a real mess of my life, because of some the choices I had made. The true picture and will of God was made plain to me. The Lord was genuinely the best thing that could or ever would happen to me, because His will was to bring out the very best in me. So that I could fulfill His preordained purpose in my life. When times were hard and those agonizing temptations seemed to clamp down on me, I was assured that I could make it if I put my trust in Him, for the Lord will bring out the best in "us" everytime.

Lesson Learned Continues

This last episode was supposed to be the knock out punch for me from Satan. He saw that I had been broken down from this yoke as low as I could possible go. How could I consider myself a Christian ever again? Satan's whole plain was devised to steal all my hopes of ever finding true love; kill my plains of having a family; and he ultimately sought to destroy the spiritual call God placed on my life. Thinking then that I would have no other choice but to serve him, because he had stopped the plain and purpose God had predestined.

What Satan didn't know was, I knew partially why I had been put in those positions. God allowed the enemy to touch me, but it was all for my good and to God's glory. I remembered in God's word that IIe says He disciplines those whom He loves. Just in knowing that I felt in my heart this assurance that God still loved me. So in the midst of my distress I remembered the, "Press to Pray to Praise."

Hebrews 12:6

6   For whom the Lord loveth he chasteneth, and scourgeth every son whom he receiveth.

One could only imagine what could happen to anyone of us, on any give day, if the Lord does not intervene.

If you would really go within yourself, examine your life, and think about all that God has done for you, how He brings you out of one circumstance, yet He carries you through another.

I know you will agree with me, "God is Majestic!" His loves goes beyond our furthest reach or call. His grace and mercy surrounds us like a radiant beam of light, which shines down upon us through His glorious sight.

The point I'm trying to make is, it doesn't matter how bad, dark, tired, and long your journey may seem. Just remember there is a lamp on your feet and the light upon your pathway should always be Jesus

Christ our Lord. As long as you never forget, "The Press to Pray to

Praise."

Through Healing and Forgiveness

I made one promise to God, I told him that if he would bless me with children I would raise them to fear him and abide by his word, and teach them all that I knew concerning him. I meant this with all of my heart, soul, and mind.

God with His infinite mercy bestowed favor upon me and blessed me to meet a wonderfully saved (born again believer) young gentleman my husband. In the beginning I was hesitant and leery of becoming friends with another male. So this time I sought the Lord **"in the prayer"** concerning my husband and I. Asking Him to lead and guide us through the development of this new friendship and enable both of us to make decisions that were pleasing, spirituality healthy, and wise in His sight. We became absolute best friends from the very beginning. I would say both of us felt blessed to had found one another. After eight months of courting we were married and our wedding was beautiful, one that you would dream of having. We sung to one another during our wedding and each lyric was sung from our hearts and souls. We thanked the Lord for the love He allowed us to find in each other, but most of all we thanked Him for the love we shared for Him.

After we were married I conceived our first child. Just to show you how low down, tricky, and bold Satan is. He tried to tempt me to abort our child. He thought that I was still abortion prone, given my past experience with this issue. The enemy would say things like, "Look at you, you just got married and you're pregnant already."

I replied, "God has blessed me with a Christian man this time, he loves God, this child, and me".

Then Satan would say, "You really don't need a baby right now, you two need to enjoy each other first, at least for one year."

I replied, "I promised God that I would never as long as I lived abort another child, plus I vowed that if He would bless me with children I would raise them to love, serve, and fear Him. Anyway I want our child, it's a gift from God."

Finally he says, "What will people think when they find out, they are going to say you were pregnant before you got married and that's why he married you anyway!"

I replied, "Satan you are a liar, God knows the truth! God has given me a second chance, I'm eternally grateful, and I shall not be moved." "Resist the devil and he must flee."

Proverbs 18:22 Who so findeth a wife findeth a **"good thing,"** and obtaineth favor of the Lord.

James 4:7

7   Submit yourselves therefore to God, Resist the devil, and he will flee from you.

Our marriage had been blessed, although I have learned through trial and error that there is no perfect marriage. I would say each pregnancy we had was untimely, unplanned, and unexpected, but graciously accepted. We seemed to always wish we had more money, yet our fund wheel never ran dry. Our father "God" had provided for us every step of the way.

God graciously blessed my spouse and I with six health children. All six were full term pregnancies with no complications. He also blessed us to sustain a full term twin pregnancy. I am compelled to say with all my heart, mind, and soul that, "God is Good!" To God be the glory for the things that he has done.

When God says He will remember your sins no more and renew your youth like an eagle. That is exactly what He means, because He gave me a new beginning. He looked past my faults, and met my every need and I bless His "Holy" name, because of it.

Psalm 103:1-5

1   Bless the LORD, O my soul: and all that is within me, bless his holy name.

2   Bless the LORD, O my soul, and forget not all his benefits:

3   Who forgiveth all thine iniquities; who healeth all thy diseases;

4   Who redeemth thy life from destruction; who crowneth thee with lovingkindness and tender mercies;

5   Who satisfieth thy mouth with good things; so that thy youth is renewed like the eagle's.

Romans 8:1

1   There is therefore now no condemnation to them which are in Christ Jesus, who walk not after the flesh, but after the Spirit.

Chapter Ten

Victims of Molestation

We hear of teenagers (male and female) missing almost everyday. When the victims are found the majority of them have been sexually abused and/or murdered. I want you to know, to recognize your blessings. If you have been abused sexually, you escaped physically, and you still have breath in your body spiritually. "Stop asking why, feeling and wish you were dead, and never say that your life is ruined because of the circumstances you have endured." Instead do the opposite, for the rest of your life praise and thank the one and only merciful God in heaven, for sparing your life through the blood of his son Jesus Christ.

Please, what ever you do don't concentrate on the incidents, issues, or mistakes you have acquired or what was done to you. First, forgive yourself, and forgive the offender. Second, find someone you genuinely trust to help guide you in putting your life back together in accordance with the word of God, and third but foremost, put all your focus and trust in the Lord. That is what He wants from each of us.

The problem, it doesn't matter, the question is can He solve them? The answer is, "Yes He Shall", just give it to him He'll bare it. How? Go some where, any place where there's only you and the Lord, lift up your head, open your mouth, and release the sorrow from your heart. Humble yourself in the presence of the LORD and He shall lift you up. Cry out to him from within your spirit. Forget about yourself and concentrate on Him. Talk to the LORD just like you are consulting in your best friend. He will hear your cry and carry your pain, because "He is more than able to deliver."

Matthew 11:28-30

28 Come unto me all ye that labor an are heavy laden, and I will give you rest.

29 Take my yoke upon you, and learn of me; for I am meek and lowly in heart: and ye shall find rest unto your souls.

30 For my yoke is easy, and my burden is light.

Psalms 121:1

1 I will lift up mine eyes unto the hills, from whence cometh my help. My help cometh from the LORD, which made heaven and earth.

PRAYER

Guidance

Psalm 25:1-7

1   Unto thee, O Lord, do I lift up my soul.

2   O my God, I trust in thee: let me not be ashamed, let not mine enemies triumph over me.

3   Yea, let none that wait on thee be ashamed: let them be ashamed which transgress without cause.

4   Shew me thy ways, O LORD; teach me thy paths.

5   Lead me in thy truth, and teach me: for thou art the God of my salvation; on thee do I wait all the day.

6   Remember, O LORD, thy tender mercies and thy lovingkindness; for they have been ever of old.

7   Remember not the sins of my youth, nor my transgression: according to thy mercy remember thou me for thy goodness sake, O LORD, In Jesus name I pray, Amen.

Endure Your Journey

I know my story may have been hard for you to believe or even imagine that this actually happened, and I hide most of these events from my family. I praise and thank the Lord for all of His blessings. He allowed me to keep my sanity, and endowed me with the strength and willingness to share this story with others.

Despite the ordeals I went through, I want you to see the majesty in God's mercy toward us even when we are guilty of faults. His powerful hand of mercy spared my life. God allowed situations to accrue but He didn't allow Satan to take my life, nor destroy my soul. He can change everything wrong, sinful, and dirty about us into something right, righteous, and holy. Justifying His decision to cleanse us through the blood of His son Jesus, therefore grants us the verdict of **"Not Guilty!"**

My teenage journey was a rough one; however, having gone through these tests and trials I am a living witness to the life changing power of God. I know without a shadow of a doubt that there is life after one has been molested and sexually abused, whether it was consensual or by force.

{There is Peace, when your pathway discloses distress in your mind, apprehension of your spirit, and oppression in your flesh, meaning your physical body. Exercise your God given Faith, when you feel all that you have thought to be true or trusted in has been waived. Hold Hope close to you when your desires and expectations make a U-turn on you and seem to be fading fast in the distance. And always Love Yourself, when it feels better to hate because of what is or has happened to you.}

For the Lord will remove the scars from within your intellectual being, and the hurt from your broken heart, and rebuild your shattered dreams. He has already replenished your self-esteem and aspirations through his redemption. Just take a stand, make a conscious decision to have the courage, and **"Endure Your Journey!"**

Chapter Eleven

Experience Speaks for Herself

Listen; believe NO ONE who says:

"There is no harm done to your body when you have an abortion, they
are safe."

Do you believe blind surgery is safe? "I could have bleed to death!"

"You will be able to have other children in the future", they say.

How would they know, are they God? God is the giver of life.

"Tomorrow is not promised to anyone!"

This is the part they don't tell you when you go to these clinics:

> The fetus may be removed violently from within your uterus
> never to return, but the scar of it's presence remains in your
> intellectual being, your mind, and in your spirit, forever never
> to be erased.

> Because mental torment, anguish, and pain from this act are
> guaranteed side effects.

"A gift is waiting for you, but it is opened early as you willed. You find it is not what you expected. So you wish you could return it marked "Please Return To Sender", unfortunately it is yours to keep, and it's there to stay" (Until the Lord rolls your pain away).

If you have been bless to escape the physical scars made to your uterus by this act, and have had other successful pregnancies, it's a miraculous thing, and you should honestly "Bless God" everyday for his mercy shown towards you.

Closing Remarks

In conclusions, I was blessed to survive and prevail over, the hurt imposed upon me during my youth by Lustful Deceit. Realizing and accepting it was never my fault (as the innocent "minor" victim) that I became Lustful Deceits "sexual pleasure."

I would like to give my summation of what Lustful Deceit did to this child: He caused her to be categorized as "damage goods" or called promiscuous, leaving upon her the spirits of deceit, lust, and fornication. Embedding within her for many years a sense of diminishing guilt and responsibly for what was unlawfully taken from her, at thirteen years of age. In addition, she adopted Lustful Deceits twisted, ruthless, and perverted false perception of love. As an effect through this dreadful experience, **her life was set in a repetitive cycle of events. She tries to restore right, for what was done wrong to her, by justifying Lustful Deceits violation of her "innocent youthful body", as deserving.**

The actions of an adult male or female verses that of a child, boy or girl can never be substantiate as being deserved or warranted by that child (victim).

For those of you who want to come to the defense of Lustful Deceit. I must warn you, don't speak to swiftly, and be very careful of what you say. With issues such as this, most people have the tendency "to choose" to ignore the truth. Failing to see that this type of abuse is totally unacceptable and unpleasing to GOD.

What happened to her could easily happen to you, your child, or relative: and possibly already has, **"you just don't know it!"** Scripture records:

When I was child, I acted like a child, I thought like a child, I reasoned like a child. When I became a man, I put my childish way behind me (NIV I Corinthians 13:11).

In other words, when it comes to the violation of a child's body, he or she can do nothing other than what they are, "react as child!" A child should never be placed in a position where he or she is expected to respond, act, or have the intellectual perceptions as that of an adult.

- Lust conceived manipulation, violation, and fornication, which brought fourth deception (lies), hurt, and devastation.

- Fornication brought forth pregnancy that produced denial of the true and more lies.

- Pregnancy and fear directed a path to abortion, guilt and shame.

- Abortion along with violation, and fornication created destruction, death and defeat.

- All equaling SIN, for the wages of sin is death.

  Lust > Fornication > Pregnancy > Abortion =SIN

Chapter Twelve

Teen Tidbits

Don't take these scriptures and my words lightly and think for one moment that just because my teenage story ended in victory, restoration, and justification yours will to, if you continue on in sin.

Romans 9:15- 17

15 For he saith to Moses, I will have mercy on whom I will have mercy, and I will have compassion on whom I will have compassion.

16 So then it is not of him that willeth, nor of him that runneth, but of God that sheweth mercy.

17 For the scripture saith unto Paraoh, Even for this same purpose have I raised thee up, that I might shew my power in thee, and that my name might be declared throughout all the earth.

I Thessalonians 4:7

7 For God hath not called us unto uncleanness, but unto holiness.

Teenagers (ladies and gentlemen) Pray to the Lord before making decisions.

Proverbs 3:6

6   In all thy ways acknowledge him, and he shall direct thy path. Trust in the Lord with all thine heart; and lean not unto thine own understanding.

All of your dreams, goal, and aspirations will be fulfilled if you put your trust in the Lord.

Matthew 6:33

33   But seek ye first the kingdom of God, and his righteousness; and all these things shall be added unto you.

Psalm 37:3-5

3   Trust in the Lord, and do good; so shalt thou dwell in the land, and verily thou shalt be fed.

4   Delight thyself also in the LORD; and he shall give thee the desires of thine heart.

5   Commit thy way unto the LORD; trust also in him; and he shall bring it to pass.

Keep yourselves until you are married if you so choose to marry, and be proud of your virginity. Respect your body first then the opposite sex will to.

I Corinthians 7:32, 34

32   But I would have you without carefulness. He that is unmarried careth for the things that belong to the Lord, how he may please the Lord.

34   There is difference also between a wife and a virgin. The unmarried woman careth for the things of the Lord, that she may be holy both in body and in spirit:

Your body is to be used for the service of God. Satan prominently uses fornication (sex) and drugs in destroying your youth.

I Corinthians 6:18-20

18   Flee fornication. Every sin that a man doeth is with out the body; but he that committeth fornication sinneth against his own body.

19   What! Know ye not that your body is the temple of the Holy Ghost which is in you, which ye have of God, and ye are not your own?

20   For ye are brought with a price: therefore glorify God in your body, and in your spirit, which are God's.

SUGGESTED DAILY PRAYER FOR A TEENAGER

NEW DAY

Good morning Lord God in heaven, Good morning Lord Jesus, Good morning Holy Ghost. Thank you Lord for allowing my family and I to live and see another day. Lord I thank you for health, strength, and all things on today. Lord I need you and I ask that you walk before me ordering my steps in your perfect will on today. Help me to overcome all hindrances, (stress, peer pressure, sex, drugs, lying, stealing, backbiting, anger, etc.. etc...) on today. Lord I seek to please only you and you alone shall I desire to serve. In your son Jesus name I pray, Amen.

STRENGTH

Lord God in heaven, I thank thee for yet another chance to come before your presence. Lord I love, honor, and adore you right now. I realize I am nothing with out you, yet I am able to do all things through your son Jesus, who strengthens me. Help me Lord to bring my flesh (thoughts, ways, wants, and desires) under subjection to the will of your spirit on today. Help me to make a conscious decision within my mind, which will transfer into my spirit on today. Therefore, making it possible for me to think only on good and acceptable things. In your son Jesus name I pray, Amen.

Memory Verses:

Philippians 4:13

13   I can do all things through Christ, which strengtheneth me.

Philippians 4:8

8   Finally, brethren, whatsoever things are true, whatsoever things are honest, whatsoever things are just, whatsoever things are pure, whatsoever things are lovely, whatsoever things are of good

report; if there be any virtue, and if there be any praise, think on these things.

Chapter Thirteen

Parental Note

Discipline, teaching our children and ourselves the necessity for suffering and the value thereof. The need to face problems directly and to experience the pain involved. Discipline is the basic set of tools we require to solve life's problems. It becomes clear that these tools are techniques of suffering, means by which we experience the pain of problems in such a way as to work them through and solve them successfully, learning and growing in the process.

When we teach ourselves and our children discipline, we are teaching them and ourselves how to suffer and also how to grow. The techniques of suffering, (meaning experiencing the pain of problems constructively) are delaying of gratification, acceptance of responsibility, dedication to truth (God) and balancing. The most vital of the four is dedication to the truth. It must continually be employed if our lives are to be healthy and our spirits are to grow. This should be obvious for truth is reality and that which is false is deceptive. The clearer we see the reality of the World the better equipped we are to deal with it's troubles.

It takes an incredible understanding of how and why people and circumstances are an important aspect of an individual's life, from birth to death; which also causes one to be open to others and to take into consideration that maybe there are underlying issues that in fact caused an individual to exhibit different levels of love, values and spiritual growth.

Love, it is not just a feeling, dependency, and the risk of commitment and attention. The experience of real love also has to do with psychological boundaries, since it involves an extension of one's limits. One's limits are one's boundaries. When we extend our limits through love, we do so by reaching out to others, and by speaking to those we love whose growth we wish to nurture. For us to be able to do this, the loved individual must first become love to us. In other words we must be attracted to, invested in, and committed to an individual outside of ourselves, beyond the boundaries of self.

Religion, spiritual growth is a journey out of the miniature world into an even greater complex universe. Religion is a journey of wisdom, knowledge, and of faith. In order to escape the miniature world of our previous experiences and free ourselves from transference's it is necessary that we learn. We must continually expand our realm of knowledge and our field of vision through the thorough digestion and annexation of new information.

So for Mental Health and Spiritual Growth we must develop our own personal relationship with God, nurture our children according to his word, and never rely on that of others.

Other Books

By Kartaysa Harris

THROUGH THE EYE OF YOUR STORM
By Kartaysa Harris

There is a time and a season for all things.
Main focus is on spiritual awareness, obtaining the ability to remain focused on what God promised for your life, and hearing God's voice in spite of the spiritual, mental, or physical storm, which stands before you.

TREASURE CHEST
By Kartaysa Harris

Inspirational readings from the heart, which inspire the soul.

WHILE YOU ARE IN THE FIRE
By Kartaysa Harris

Behind enemy lines, but he shall not over take thee.
Remain steadfast, unmovable, believing that God is with you always even until the end of the World.

In Loving Memory

"The Three"

I can never replace you,

But the memory of you has never left

my mind,

No matter how much I wish,

I could turn back the tables of time,

God has given me peace in knowing,

That you are all safe in His loving

arms,

I mark this book as your birth

records,

In acknowledgment that all three of

you did exist,

I will forever share my experience,

with those who still persist.

Kartaysa T. Berry Harris

About the Author

Evangelist Kartaysa Harris is the author of, Through the Eye of Your Storm, Treasure Chest, and While You Are in The Fire. She and husband, Darwin, have been married thirteen years and have six children. She enjoys spending time with her family, singing, sewing, instructing, and interacting, with young people.

CPSIA information can be obtained
at www.ICGtesting.com
Printed in the USA
BVHW071913011019
559928BV00001B/98/P